MW01240927

A compilation of

120

NUGGETS OF WISDOM

FOR LIFE

Dr. Angela M. Rucker

ALEGNA PRESS

Alegna Press
P.O. Box 7174
Largo, MD 20792
Phone: 301-883-2121

Published by Alegna Press 10/12/2022

ISBN: 9798357496379

Scripture taken from The Holy Bible, King James Version. Public Domain

The book is printed on acid-free paper.

Author's Contact

Dr. Angela M. Rucker

Angela Rucker Ministries
International (ARMI)
P.O. Box 7174
Largo, MD 20792, USA

Email: armintl1126@gmail.com

Other books by the Author:

The Pre-Natal Assignment:
A Journey into your Prophetic Destiny

Breaking Forth:
A Release into your Kairos Season

Self Check

"And the Lord said,

My spirit shall not

always strive with man,

for that he also is flesh;

yet his days shall be an

hundred and twenty

years"

Genesis 6:3

Acknowledgements

To Almighty God who makes something out of nothing.

To my wonderful co-laborers in the gospel at Bride of Christ Church Ministries International. Thank you for your awesome display of servanthood. It is a great honor to co-labor with you.

I am forever grateful to Dr. Geneva Henderson whose loyalty still amazes me. Dr. Alan Johnson, I thank you for multitasking and for your labor of love. Pastor Emmanuel Falodun, I remain grateful for your help with this project and the many ways you allow God to use you. To my amazing husband, Apostle Benjamin Rucker, thank you for all you do to make it happen for me. Thank you for loving me enough to push me into my destiny.

A note from the Author

It is impossible to do what is right without instructions. There is a process of development that is required for maturity to be evident. Instructions without application foster stagnation and compel you to remain in an existing state.

Self Check presents a compilation of one hundred and twenty instructional nuggets that are the offspring of communion and devotion. Each nugget prompts you to observe and practice disciplined principles to help you ascend beyond where you are. The instructions beckon you to enter a chamber of wisdom that reshapes your thinking and transforms your habits.

Self Check ignites the fight in you to press your way out of the cocoon to become the person you are destined to be.

ONE

Yesterday is over and today is the beginning of many fantastic new opportunities. No matter how complex your past has been, you can begin again. Do not focus on the failures of yesterday. Start your day with great expectations of a glorious future. You will find a new direction if you let the hand of God carry you. Leave the comfort of the shore and sail out toward the horizon of your destiny. It is never too late to become who you want to be. Let today be the beginning of a brand new you!

"Remember ye not the former things, neither consider the things of old. Behold, I will do a new thing; now it shall spring forth; shall ye not know it? I will even make a way in the wilderness, and rivers in the desert." Isaiah 43:18-19 (KJV)

TWO

Take time to care for yourself. In your giving out, remember to stop and refill. An empty soul cannot give what it does not have. Love you enough to take care of yourself. Learn how to pour out and refill. Care for others but do not forget to pamper yourself.

"Take my yoke upon you and learn of me; for I am meek and lowly in heart: and ye shall find rest unto your souls." Matthew 11:29 (KJV)

THREE

Stop going along with the crowd. There is a leader in you that needs to be unveiled. Be the Standard Bearer and the World Changer. Wave your flag of influence boldly to impact others for the Kingdom of God. Set the temperature of the environment and do not adjust to the climate of the crowd. Be different!

"Ye are the salt of the earth: but if the salt have lost his savor, wherewith shall it be salted? it is thenceforth good for nothing, but to be cast out, and to be trodden under foot of men. Ye are the light of the world."
Matthew 5:13-14 (KJV)

FOUR

Do not panic when there are sudden shifts in your life. Your future is history with God. He knows the pre-designed course to your destiny. He knows how to shift things around to get you to where you need to be. He will move people, cancel plans, and change your options. Just be willing to adjust your perspective, take an intentional pause, and hit the reset button. Trust God!

"Commit thy way unto the LORD; trust also in him; and he shall bring it to pass." Psalm 37:5 (KJV)

FIVE

Laugh your way through your day. When you laugh you remove yourself from being a victim to a victor. Laughter is contagious; it is a blessing to others and is medicine for your soul. Maturity is when you can laugh at yourself while you learn from your mistakes. Let your day be a day of laughter!

"A merry heart doeth good like a medicine: but a broken spirit dries the bones·" Proverbs 17:22 (KJV)

SIX

Worry is a threat to wholesomeness. Do not spend your time worrying about what could or might happen. Purge your mind of every imagination that fosters doom and gloom. Trying to climb imaginary mountains of problems will keep you crippled in depression. Trust God...He is The Waymaker!

"Be careful for nothing; but in everything by prayer and supplication with thanksgiving let your requests be made known unto God· And the peace of God, which passeth all understanding, shall keep your hearts and minds through Christ Jesus·"
Philippians 4:6-8 (KJV)

SEVEN

Change your attitude and you can change your life. Choose to fly high even when the wind of adversity is blowing against you. Airplanes take off against the wind. Eagles use the wind of the storm to soar to great heights. Use your storm to lift you higher. The problem is not the storm, but your attitude about the storm. Rejoice!

"This is the day which the Lord hath made; we will rejoice and be glad in it." Psalm 118:24 (KJV)

EIGHT

There are times when you feel like you are not sure about your next step. You simply must dig deep and step out with confidence into the unknown. Do not be distracted by the noise around you. Keep stepping and do not look back. Each step takes you closer to your victory. Let God be your compass. Step out in faith.

"For we walk by faith, not by sight." 2 Corinthians 5:7 (KJV)

NINE

Dismiss your fears and open the door to courage. Do not be afraid to embrace something new or different. It was not professionals who built the ark; they built the titanic that sank. God used amateurs to build the ark of safety. Feed your courage and your fears will starve to death.

"The Lord is on my side; I will not fear." Psalm 118:6 (KJV)

TEN

Do not give up because it did not happen yesterday. Do not get stuck in the past. Stay in the race and try again today. It does not matter how long it takes you to get there so long as you keep going. Quitters never get to the end of the road. Perseverance is the road to your destiny.

"Brethren, I count not myself to have apprehended: but this one thing I do, forgetting those things which are behind, and reaching forth unto those things which are before, I press toward the mark for the prize of the high calling of God in Christ Jesus." Philippians 3:13-14 (KJV)

ELEVEN

If you follow the crowd, you will always be a part of the crowd. Your uniqueness is God's gift to you. Your special qualities can take you beyond the limits of the crowd to your destiny.
Dare to be different!

"For we are his workmanship, created in Christ Jesus unto good works, which God hath before ordained that we should walk in them."
Ephesians 2:10 (KJV)

TWELVE

Success does not come by wishful thinking. It requires a change of heart not just mind over matter. Desire is the key to motivation, but it takes determination, focus, commitment, dedication, self-discipline, and action. The journey can transform us from who we are to who we can become.

"…be ye transformed by the renewing of your mind, that ye may prove what is that good, and acceptable, and perfect, will of God."
Romans 12:2 (KJV)

THIRTEEN

Initiative releases the power that is locked inside of you. You exercise faith when you are willing to take a stand, take risks, take responsibility, and move into action. Initiative is an act of faith. It is good to do the right thing without being told.

"Even so faith if it hath not works, is dead, being alone· Yea, a man may say, Thou hast faith, and I have works: shew me thy faith without thy works, and I will shew thee my faith by my works·"
James 2:17-18 (KJV)

FOURTEEN

Are you facing challenges in your life that appear too difficult to overcome? Do not allow the walls that stand in your way to separate you from your destiny. You must be passionate and have a burning desire to possess all that God has for you. Walls are not there to keep you out. They are there so you can show how badly you want to get in. With faith, you can tear down every wall that rises against you.

"So the people shouted when the priests blew with the trumpets: and it came to pass, when the people heard the sound of the trumpet, and the people shouted with a great shout, that the wall fell down flat, so that the people went up into the city, every man straight before him, and they took the city." Joshua 6:20 (KJV)

14

FIFTEEN

Be willing to step away from the port of familiar shores to discover new worlds. A comfort zone mentality will not allow you to see beyond the horizon. Comfortability is the enemy of progress and a deterrent to purpose.

"I can do all things through Christ that strengtheneth me."
Philippians 4:13 (KJV)

SIXTEEN

Clutter prevents you from seeing and thinking clearly and it blocks your understanding. Get rid of those unwanted thoughts. Clearing the clutter in your life -- be it physical, mental, emotional, or spiritual -- gets rid of confusion and ushers in the peace of God.

"But let all things be done decently and in order."
1 Corinthians 14:40 (KJV)

SEVENTEEN

Today affords you the opportunity to start over. Yesterday's failures can be today's achievements. Just because you failed yesterday, doesn't mean you're going to fail today. Do not allow your past to sabotage your present. Rise up, release yourself from the shackles of your past, and start over.

"Brethren, I count not myself to have apprehended: but this one thing I do, forgetting those things which are behind, and reaching forth unto those things which are before, I press toward the mark for the prize of the high calling of God in Christ Jesus." Philippians 3:13-14 (KJV)

EIGHTEEN

Promise yourself to rise above mediocrity. Do not major in minors. Consider things that are meaningful and purposeful. Do not give thought to anything that does not line up with the Word of God. Excuse yourself from efforts that bring no gain and add no value to your life.

"Finally, brethren, whatsoever things are true, whatsoever things are honest, whatsoever things are just, whatsoever things are pure, whatsoever things are lovely, whatsoever things are of good report; if there be any virtue, and if there be any praise, think on these things." Philippians 4:8 (KJV)

ℛℐℕℰ𝒯ℰℰℕ

It is good to be happy but happiness can never afford you what joy brings. Happiness comes with interruptions, but the joy of the Lord is a constant source of bliss. Joy is found in the presence of God. Do not stop at 'Happy'... go for JOY!

"For the kingdom of God is not meat and drink; but righteousness, and peace, and joy in the Holy Ghost." Romans 14:17 (KJV)

TWENTY

Learn to smile through adversity. Challenges allow you to dig deep within yourself and release the power inside. Your smile does not say that you do not hurt...it says you have the power to overcome the pain. Adversity prepares ordinary people for an extraordinary destiny!

"Ye are of God, little children, and have overcome them: because greater is he that is in you, than he that is in the world." 1 John 4:4 (KJV)

TWENTY-ONE

Making decisions without seeking wise counsel can lead to disaster. Utilize the wisdom of those who are walking upright before the Lord.

"Where no counsel is, the people fall: but in the multitude of counselors there is safety."
Proverbs 11:14 (KJV)

TWENTY-TWO

Be careful of Spiritual Indigestion. You cannot eat off every table. Some dishes may not be good for you. Who recommended the chef? If you are on a special diet, you cannot eat everything that is presented to you.

"Beloved, believe not every spirit, but try the spirits whether they are of God: because many false prophets are gone out into the world."
1 John 4:1 (KJV)

22

TWENTY-THREE

Motivation will get you started but when you are fully persuaded you keep on going. Your success is not based on what others think...it is based on what you conceive in your mind. When you are fully persuaded in your mind, nothing can stop you from achieving.

"One man esteemeth one day above another: another esteemeth every day alike· Let every man be fully persuaded in his own mind·"
Romans 14:5 (KJV)

TWENTY-FOUR

As long as there is life, there is hope. No matter what you are going through, hold on to hope. Do not give up! Your circumstance is temporary and it will change. Hold on to God's unchanging hand and He will lead you to victory.

"We are troubled on every side, yet not distressed; we are perplexed, but not in despair; Persecuted, but not forsaken; cast down, but not destroyed"
2 Corinthians 4:8-9 (KJV)

TWENTY-FIVE

When you focus on reshaping and improving your own life, you will have no time to criticize and demean others.

"And why beholdest thou the mote that is in thy brother's eye, but considerest not the beam that is in thine own eye? Or how wilt thou say to thy brother, let me pull out the mote out of thine eye; and behold, a beam is in thine own eye? Thou hypocrite, first cast out the beam out of thine own eye; and then shalt thou see clearly to cast out the mote out of thy brother's eye."
Matthew 7:3-5 (KJV)

TWENTY-SIX

Do not use anything in a battle that you have not tested and proven. So many of us lose the fight because we are using weapons that we have not tested. It is not one size fits all...you must find the perfect fit. When God anoints you for the assignment, the fit is perfect.

"And David girded his sword upon his armor, and he assayed to go; for he had not proved it. And David said unto Saul, I cannot go with these; for I have not proved them. And David put them off him."
1 Samuel 17:39 (KJV)

TWENTY-SEVEN

Where are you going? Are you heading toward or away from God's purpose for your life? Use God's Positioning System (GPS) to direct you to the right path.

"I will instruct thee and teach thee in the way which thou shalt go I will guide thee with mine eye."
Psalm 32:8 (KJV)

TWENTY-EIGHT

Ok...so just because you fell off the horse does not mean you cannot get back on it. Learn from your mistake and keep on riding. Each mistake is an opportunity for you to learn how to be a better rider.

"For a just man falleth seven times, and riseth up again."
Proverbs 24:16 (KJV)

28

TWENTY-NINE

Doubts are born in the middle of any journey and the struggle to the finish line is real. Do not abort the vision. Do not ever allow your present circumstance to cause you to forfeit your victory. Keep pressing through. The faith in your heart must be stronger than the doubt in your mind. God will perfect everything that concerns you. His grace will carry you to the end.

"And he said unto me, my grace is sufficient for thee: for my strength is made perfect in weakness."
2 Corinthians 12:9 (KJV)

THIRTY

Just because you make reference to someone's name does not mean you know and have a relationship with the person. Name dropping does not guarantee you an entrance.

"Many will say to me in that day, Lord, Lord, have we not prophesied in thy name? and in thy name have cast out devils? and in thy name done many wonderful works? And then will I profess unto them, I never knew you: depart from me, ye that work iniquity."
Matthew 7:22-23 (KJV)

THIRTY-ONE

Not every way is the right way. Know where you are going before you start the journey. Choose right and you will never end up being wrong.

"There is a way which seemeth right unto a man, but the end thereof are the ways of death."
Proverbs 14:12 (KJV)

THIRTY-TWO

When your life is submitted to the will of God, you can expect the favor of God to surround you.

"For the LORD God is a sun and shield; the LORD will give grace, and glory: No good thing will He withhold from them that walk uprightly."
Psalm 84:11 (KJV)

THIRTY-THREE

If you stay in your lane there will be no mishaps. When you illegally occupy a place outside of your divine jurisdiction, your labor will be in vain. Find your spot!

"Now there are diversities of gifts, but the same Spirit. And there are differences of administrations, but the same Lord. And there are diversities of operations, but it is the same God which worketh all in all. But the manifestation of the Spirit is given to every man to profit withal."
1 Corinthians 12:4-7 (KJV)

THIRTY-FOUR

Maximize your time. It is a fleeting commodity that will expire. You will never get back time that is lost. Exercise good stewardship. Take advantage of it NOW!

"I must work the works of him that sent me, while it is day: the night cometh, when no man can work."
John 9:4 (KJV)

THIRTY-FIVE

Let the Word of God be a garrison around you. Protect yourself from enemy invasion. The enemy plans to rob you of everything that God has set aside for you. Be watchful!

"The thief cometh not, but for to steal, and to kill, and to destroy. I am come that they might have life, and that they might have it more abundantly." John 10:10 (KJV)

THIRTY-SIX

You will meet great resistance when you step into purpose. Focus on purpose and you will overcome the resistance. You were born to accommodate purpose in the face of adversity. God's got you!

"When thou passeth through the waters, I will be with thee; and through the rivers, they shall not overflow thee: when thou walkest through the fire, thou shalt not be burned, neither shall the flame kindle upon thee." Isaiah 43:2 (KJV)

THIRTY-SEVEN

The internet can give you information about geography, economy, science, and culture but it cannot give you information about your destiny. God is the designer of your prophetic destiny. He will never misguide you. If you follow His lead, you will never end up at a dead end!

"Then spake Jesus again unto them, saying, I am the light of the world: he that followeth me shall not walk in darkness, but shall have the light of life." John 8:12 (KJV)

THIRTY-EIGHT

Triumph at the top of the mountain is often preceded by anguish in the valley. Pain is a prerequisite to personal achievement. The journey to your destiny is punctuated by tests and trials. Press through!

"My brethren, count it all joy when ye fall into divers temptations; Knowing this, that the trying of your faith worketh patience."
James 1:2-3 (KJV)

THIRTY-NINE

Learning how to embrace the unknown ushers you into a higher realm of trust in God.

"For we walk by faith, not by sight." 2 Corinthians 5:7 (KJV)

FORTY

Spiritual insight allows you to see beyond what is in front of you to what is ahead of you. The Holy Spirit corrects nearsightedness (myopia) and gives you discernment so you can see beyond where you look.

"Open thou mine eyes, that I may behold wondrous things out of thy law." Psalm 119:18 (KJV)

FORTY-ONE

Whenever you tolerate fear you deactivate courage. Conquer your fear by doing that which you fear to do. Fear is the enemy's weapon that is used against your mind to paralyze you and make you impotent. Evict fear from your mind.

"For God hath not given us the spirit of fear; but of power, and of love, and of a sound mind."
2 Timothy 1:7 (KJV)

FORTY-TWO

Arise!!!
Do not allow your circumstance to pull you down and under. If you think you are defeated, you will be. You cannot rise above the level of your thoughts. Command adversity to bow to you. Your destiny is above and not beneath.

"And the Lord shall make thee the head, and not the tail; and thou shalt be above only···and thou shalt not be beneath."
Deuteronomy 28:13 (KJV)

FORTY-THREE

You will never get any further than where you are if you stay where you are!

"I press toward the mark for the prize of the high calling of God in Christ Jesus."
Philippians 3:14 (KJV)

FORTY-FOUR

Sometimes you must leave a place of comfort for a place of discomfort. When God is repositioning you for greatness, you must endure the pain for gain. Your present situation will not be your destination. Trust God through the transition!

"Behold, I have graven thee upon the palms of my hands; thy walls are continually before me."
Isaiah 49:16 (KJV)

FORTY-FIVE

We need to stop making promises and not keeping them. It is best not to say anything than to say 'yes' and you do 'no.' It shows a lack of integrity when we say we are going to do something and choose not to do it. Keep your word at any cost!

"But let your communication be, Yea, yea; Nay, nay: for whatsoever is more than these cometh of evil."
Matthew 5:37 (KJV)

FORTY-SIX

Work on expanding your spiritual intelligence. We need authentic power found in knowledge, wisdom, and truth which comes from the Holy Ghost. It is more than a shout and a dance!

"Howbeit when He, the Spirit of truth, is come, He will guide you into all truth: for He shall not speak of Himself;··· But the Advocate, the Holy Spirit, whom the Father will send in My name, will teach you all things·" John 16:13 (KJV)

FORTY-SEVEN

When things fall apart, do not give up on your dream. Just because you failed, it is no reason for you to accept defeat. Failure is temporary, but defeat is permanent.
You can sprout again!

"For there is hope of a tree if it is cut down, that it will sprout again, and that the tender branch thereof will not cease." Job 14:7 (KJV)

FORTY-EIGHT

Fix your heart to praise God. Move out of the way and give God the praises He deserves. It was God who woke you up this morning and not you. Praise Him for who He is. Praise Him just because He is God!

"My heart is fixed, O God, my heart is fixed: I will sing and give praise. Awake up, my glory; awake, psaltery and harp: I will awake early. I will praise thee, O Lord, among the people: I will sing unto thee among the nations." Psalm 57: 7-9 (KJV)

FORTY-NINE

You have the power and authority from the 'Supreme Court' to annihilate any activity that threatens your destiny. Heaven has declared that you can cancel every subversive plan of attack against you. Arise and take dominion!

"Behold, I give unto you power to tread on serpents and scorpions, and over all the power of the enemy: and nothing shall by any means hurt you." Luke 10:19 (KJV)

FIFTY

Self-examination is an effective way to address the soul. That which we dread on the outside of us could very well live on the inside. The faults we find in others often mirror our weaknesses. Never be found guilty of profession without possession. Search your soul!

"Examine yourselves, whether ye be in the faith; prove your own selves. Know ye not your own selves."
2 Corinthians 13:5 (KJV)

FIFTY-ONE

Go back and finish what you started. Do not quit the journey before you arrive at the destination. Your victory is in the finish!

"Jesus saith unto them, My meat is to do the will of him that sent me, and to finish his work."
John 4:34 (KJV)

FIFTY-TWO

When you find your 'WHY', it makes it impossible for you to merely exist. Finding it arouses the passion in you to live a life of accomplishments. Living for something is more important than just existing. Talent which does not find purpose stays buried in mediocrity.

"For we are his workmanship, created in Christ Jesus unto good works, which God hath before ordained that we should walk in them."
Ephesians 2:10 (KJV)

FIFTY-THREE

It is not about what went wrong. Focus on the endless possibilities to make things right. Do not let your past rob you of your future. God says you are more than a conqueror. Rise and conquer everything that threatens your destiny.

"Nay, in all these things we are more than conquerors through him that loved us." Romans 8:37 (KJV)

FIFTY-FOUR

When you keep going around in circles and making the same mistakes, it is time to confront and correct yourself. It is not about the people you interact with daily. It is about the person looking back at you in the mirror. If you spend your time looking for the faults in others, you will have no time to recognize and correct your faults.

Search me, O God, and know my heart: try me, and know my thoughts: And see if there be any wicked way in me and lead me in the way everlasting.
Psalm 139:23-24 (KJV)

FIFTY-FIVE

Stop making excuses about having no time to be with people you say you care about. It is not about having time. It is about making time if they matter to you.

"Look not every man on his own things, but every man also on the things of others."
Philippians 2:4 (KJV)

FIFTY-SIX

Never concede to failure but be confident in what you do. The difficulty that you face brings out the best in you. Face adversity with courage and command it to bow. Do not be deterred by the wall you might be facing. You have the capacity to bring that wall down. Victory comes to those who press on against the odds. Failure begins in the mind. You were born a champion, a warrior, one who defied the odds by winning the most gruesome battle of them all -- the race to the egg in your mother's womb. You can still win!

"Know ye not that they which run in a race run all, but one receiveth the prize? So run, that ye may obtain." 1 Corinthians 9:24 (KJV)

FIFTY-SEVEN

Disappointments are a part of life. The disappointment can be crushing but it is not the end of your story. Whenever you are moving toward your destiny, there will always be obstacles, mistakes, and setbacks along the way. But do not camp out in the valley of despair. Reset and begin again. Be more determined to achieve your goal. With hard work, perseverance, and faith in God, there is no limit to what you can achieve. On those days when it feels like your world has come crashing down around you, remember this: you can rise again to follow your dream. There is always a way to victory. It is not what happens to you...it is what you choose to become. Dig deep!

"But thanks be to God, which giveth us the victory through our Lord Jesus Christ." 1 Corinthians 15:57 (KJV)

FIFTY-EIGHT

Learn to embrace change. To experience life is to experience change. The caterpillar would never have been transformed into a beautiful butterfly if it rejected change. The fear of the unknown can cause us to reject newness and we never get to see the other side of life. Letting go and letting God gives us the greater strength that will allow us to embrace change.

Get ready for the shift!

"Behold, I will do a new thing; now it shall spring forth; shall ye not know it? I will even make a way in the wilderness, and rivers in the desert." Isaiah 43:19 (KJV)

FIFTY-NINE

Be encouraged today!
So what if you tried and failed? Do not worry about the many times you failed. Worry about the chances you missed because of the many times you did not try. Failure defeats losers but it inspires winners. See your failure as a teacher and not an undertaker. A detour is not a dead end, it is just another way to get to where you are going. If you do nothing you will always be defeated. Successful people are defined by how well they rise from failing. Try Again!

"I press toward the mark for the prize of the high calling of God in Christ Jesus."
Philippians 3:14 (KJV)

SIXTY

If some people in your space want to leave you, let them go. The space around you is essential for your growth. Protect it at all costs. A flame is only as great as the air it consumes. When your standards are high, those who are merely taking up space will fall away. LET THEM GO!

"Keep thy heart with all diligence; for out of it are the issues of life."
Proverbs 4:23 (KJV)

SIXTY-ONE

Sometimes we say things and do not care about the effect it has on others. Your words have more power than atom bombs. Words have the multipurpose incredible ability to do so many things. Words can be used to help, heal, compliment, criticize, hurt, harm, and humiliate. The tongue has no bones but is strong enough to break a heart. Words used today can sustain wounds ten years later. Only words that build up should be said. Criticism should be done whereby it brings grace to the hearer. WATCH WHAT YOU SAY!

"Let no corrupt communication proceed out of your mouth, but that which is good to the use of edifying, that it may minister grace unto the hearers."
Ephesians 4:29 (KJV)

SIXTY-TWO

You can be changed by the truth but you will never be reduced by it. Accept no one's definition of you. Only God can define you. When you are content to be simply yourself and not compare or compete, you will embrace the value of the masterpiece God has created and defined.

"I will praise thee; for I am fearfully and wonderfully made: marvellous are thy works; and that my soul knoweth right well·"
Psalm 139:14 (KJV)

SIXTY-THREE

When you seek approval from people, you set yourself up for rejection. Man cannot disapprove what God has already approved!

"For do I now persuade men, or God? or do I seek to please men? for if I yet pleased men, I should not be the servant of Christ."
Galatians 1:10 (KJV)

SIXTY-FOUR

Greed is a heart issue. It is a self-destructive force in an endless effort to get yours plus what everyone else has. It is the unsatisfied soul that has an excessive desire for gain and is never grateful for the blessings of God.

"And he said unto them, Take heed, and beware of covetousness: for a man's life consisteth not in the abundance of the things which he possesseth." Luke 12:15 (KJV)

SIXTY-FIVE

Learn how to stay away from people who demean your value and destroy your image. Do not give them permission to define you. Just remember who you are from God's perspective. If you focus on being the person God created you to be, you will not have to worry about living up to the expectations of other people. When you know who you truly are, the need to compare yourself to others becomes highly unnecessary.

"Fear ye not therefore, ye are of more value than many sparrows."
Matthew 10:31 (KJV)

SIXTY-SIX

Do not settle for the sky being your limit when there are footsteps on the moon. Free yourself from self-imposed boundaries. Figure out what your purpose is; then be willing to make the sacrifice to achieve it.

Go for it!

"I can do all things through Christ which strengtheneth me."
Philippians 4:13 (KJV)

SIXTY-SEVEN

Be not paralyzed by the obstacles life throws your way. Look at setbacks and challenges as ways to learn more about your hidden strength. Just as the butterfly struggles to evolve into newness, your struggles will pass and you will break through into a future that is better than your past.
Keep moving!

"For I, the LORD thy God will hold thy right hand, saying unto thee, Fear not; I will help thee."
Isaiah 41:13 (KJV)

SIXTY-EIGHT

Unless you get rid of baggage from the past, you will never maximize the new season. You cannot embrace what is before you if you keep holding on to what is behind you. The baggage of your past will hinder you from stepping into your future.
Dump it!

"Brethren, I count not myself to have apprehended: but this one thing I do, forgetting those things which are behind, and reaching forth unto those things which are before, I press toward the mark for the prize of the high calling of God in Christ Jesus." Philippians 3:13-14 (KJV)

SIXTY-NINE

One of the great detriments to successful living is slothfulness. To meander through life and think one day is just as good as the other is the way of the sluggard. Tomorrow should not be held hostage because of the inadequacies of today. Maximize today and not live life postponing things that we can do today for tomorrow. When we operate in slothfulness, we are ignorant of the value of time or the meaning of seasons.

"Go to the ant, thou sluggard; consider her ways, and be wise: Which having no guide, overseer, or ruler, provideth her meat in the summer, and gathereth her food in the harvest. How long wilt thou sleep, O sluggard? when wilt thou arise out of thy sleep?" Proverbs 6:6-9 (KJV)

SEVENTY

Fear is a debilitating weight that must be removed from our lives. It is a weapon used by the enemy to separate us from our purpose. Ignorance is the parent of fear and insecurity is its offspring. When we allow fear to dominate our lives, we give it authority to effectually rob our minds of the ability to think correctly. Fear summons you to 'Forget Everything and Run' but when you unload fear you can 'Face Everything and Rise.' Living with fear prohibits you from taking risks and if you never go out on a limb you will never get to the fruit. Do not fear failure so much that you refuse to go beyond the unknown.

"Fear thou not; for I am with thee: be not dismayed; for I am thy God: I will strengthen thee; yea, I will help thee; yea, I will uphold thee with the right hand of my righteousness." Isaiah 41:10 (KJV)

SEVENTY-ONE

One of the greatest traitors of the mind is Doubt. It is a deceptive tool that the enemy uses to make us lack confidence in the truth. Doubt has the capacity to kill more dreams than failure. Doubting God is the trap that the enemy sets so that we can sabotage our destiny and live a life of defeat. If the enemy can get his foot in the door by making us Doubt, the rest of his plan can quickly follow. Faith is the antithesis of Doubt. With faith we can move mountains -- with Doubt we create mountains. When we fill our minds with God's Word, we are unable to be affected by Doubt.

"But let him ask in faith, nothing wavering. For he, that wavereth is like a wave of the sea driven with the wind and tossed."
James 1:6 (KJV)

SEVENTY-TWO

Of all the traps and pitfalls in life, low self-esteem is the deadliest, and the hardest to overcome. It is a pit created by your own mind. It creates a distorted image of self that causes you to become a slave to the opinions of others. Low self-esteem causes you to live in a world of isolation and devaluation. When you have a good opinion of yourself, you will not try to get validation and attention from other people. When you embrace the truth that you are fearfully and wonderfully made by God, you will recognize how significant and valuable you are.

"I will praise thee; for I am fearfully and wonderfully made: marvellous are thy works; and that my soul knoweth right well."
Psalm 139:14 (KJV)

SEVENTY-THREE

The only thing standing between you and your goal is an excuse. You keep making excuses for your failure. Unload all your excuses and go after what you want in life. Hold yourself responsible to a higher standard than anyone else expects of you and do not excuse yourself from achieving your goals. The excuse trap is an ambush set by the enemy to derail you from living your purpose. Stop making excuses for who and where you are. Create positive momentum and keep on moving toward your goals. It is within your power to make great things happen.

"And they all with one consent began to make excuse. The first said unto him, I have bought a piece of ground, and I must needs go and see it: I pray thee have me excused." Luke 14:18 (KJV)

SEVENTY-FOUR

A life that is governed by deception rejects truth. The greatest deception is to deceive self. Deception causes you to forfeit the confidence of people in your sphere of influence and to lose their respect. Deception is the way of liars and it will never outlast the truth. It is a way out for those who seek to gain by being dishonest. Deception lives in the heart and it blocks the flow of goodness. It locks you in a cage of fear and prevents you from being authentic. It is a cancer of the mind that distorts your thinking and causes you to live a lie.

"Be not deceived; God is not mocked: for whatsoever a man soweth, that shall he also reap." Galatians 6:7 (KJV)

SEVENTY-FIVE

Anger shrinks you while forgiveness forces you to grow beyond what you are. When anger consumes the mind, it directs a course of action that welcomes irrational behavior which leads to regret. Anger is a valid emotion but it is bad when it takes control and makes you do things you do not want to do. Anger is an acid that can do more harm to the vessel in which it is stored than to anything on which it is poured. Never make permanent decisions when you are angry. When you harbor anger, it damages your soul. Anger is one letter short of danger.

"Cease from anger and forsake wrath: fret not thyself in any wise to do evil." Psalm 37:8 (KJV)

SEVENTY-SIX

Strife is another trick that the enemy uses to rob us of peace and to keep us entangled in our petty disagreements, disappointments, and disputes. It is impossible to enjoy the peace of God when there is strife. Wherever there is strife, there is always that unteachable spirit of pride. Someone bent on strife will not allow compromise, negotiation, or humility. Strife alienates friends, divides families, destroys churches, and causes people to abandon visions. God hates strife and He has commanded us in His word to avoid strife.

"A froward man soweth strife: and a whisperer separateth chief friends."
Proverbs 16:28 (KJV)

SEVENTY-SEVEN

Disorganization ushers in confusion and clutter that prevent us from operating at a level of excellence. The Bible admonishes us to do everything in decency and order. Disorganization is a weapon of mass destruction that the enemy uses against the people of God to confuse them and render them useless. For us to be effective, our lives must be organized. Clutter promotes confusion and blocks our focus. The hallmark of a disorganized individual is unfinished business. They never finish what they start.

"For God is not the author of confusion, but of peace, as in all churches of the saints."
1 Corinthians 14:33 (KJV)

SEVENTY-EIGHT

Impatience is a self-destructive tool. Trusting God requires that we patiently embrace God's sovereignty and allow His perfect will to unfold in our lives. Impatience is a hindrance that is designed to rob you of your peace, keep you in the dungeon of anxiety and confuse your thoughts. When we are impatient, we attempt to take shortcuts that can derail the path to our destiny. It causes wise people to act foolishly. Impatience has ruined many crowns; it has lured many people to give up when they have just a few minutes to win, just a few millimeters to cross the finish line. Impatience causes us to settle for spurts of temporary happiness instead of steadfast unspeakable joy.

"Wait on the LORD: be of good courage, and he shall strengthen thine heart: wait, I say, on the LORD."
Psalm 27:14 (KJV)

SEVENTY-NINE

Gluttony is a great hindrance to our wellbeing. It is another deceptive tool that the enemy uses to help us to self-destruct. Gluttony is symptomatic of deep inward struggles that we fail to resolve. Excessive eating is a panacea that is often used to relieve deep-rooted hurts and pain. If we are unable to control our eating habits, we are also unable to control other habits, such as those of the mind (lust, covetousness, anger), and unable to manage other areas of our lives. Gluttony distorts your perception of reality and damages your ability to recognize the underlying cause of the dissatisfaction that leads to overindulgence and the path to self-destruction.

"And put a knife to thy throat if thou be a man given to appetite."
Proverbs 23:2 (KJV)

EIGHTY

Rebellion always begins in the heart. Rebellion against God's authority was humanity's first sin and continues to be our downfall. Our sinful natures do not want to bow to the authority of another, even God. Disobedience is the offspring of rebellion and is the seed of unrighteousness. Wherever you find rebellion, pride has gone before and blazed the path. Rebellion goes against the order of God and vehemently protests by engaging in behaviors that are against the Word of God. The spirit of rebellion is a treacherous root that must be exposed and uprooted for us to please God.

"For rebellion is as the sin of witchcraft, and stubbornness is as iniquity and idolatry. Because thou hast rejected the word of the LORD, he hath also rejected thee from being king." 1 Samuel 15:23 (KJV)

EIGHTY-ONE

Apathy is a spiritual numbness that creeps in and corrupts our thoughts and prevents us from having the passion to excel in life. It robs us of our zeal to conquer and we become indifferent to mediocrity. Apathy is a risk aversion mentality that rejects going beyond our present state to arrive at better. Apathy is the acceptance of the unacceptable and is evident when there is no moral or spiritual compass. It thwarts our objectivity and causes us to forsake good for evil. Apathy destroys your soul, allows you to dry rot, and hinders you from being all that God has called you to be.

"Be watchful, and strengthen the things which remain, that are ready to die: for I have not found thy works perfect before God." Revelation 3:2 (KJV)

EIGHTY-TWO

Lying is a sin and is displeasing to God. A person who lies misrepresents Christ and is not a credible witness. God hates lying but He delights in those who tell the truth. Lying is the work of the devil who the Bible identifies as the father of lies. Lying is the opposite of truth and whether a small lie or a big lie, it is sin before God. Lying forces you to exist in a world of falsehood, dishonesty, and distorted reality. A lie does not have to be verbalized but is told by your behavior and your lifestyle. Lying by omission occurs when an important fact is left out to foster a misconception. Lying in any form is a sin against God and it puts our relationship with God in jeopardy.

"Keep thy tongue from evil, and thy lips from speaking guile."
Psalm 34:13 (KJV)

EIGHTY-THREE

Life comes with so many uncertainties but in the midst of it all, God is our certainty and He gives us peace. Peace is not the absence of conflict; it is the ability to remain calm amid conflict and chaos. An eye for an eye will only make the whole world blinded. When the power of love overcomes the love of power, peace will reign in our hearts. Peace comes from within. To seek it on the outside will subjugate you to the will of others. Life is too short to spend our time in turmoil and conflict. Every restless heart can find peace through God. Let God in and allow Him to rearrange the contents of your heart.

"Thou wilt keep him in perfect peace, whose mind is stayed on thee: because he trusteth in thee."
Isaiah 26:3 (KJV)

EIGHTY-FOUR

Let us be grateful for the people who are good to us. We must find time to stop and show gratefulness for those who make a difference in our lives. Do not take for granted the kindness that they show. When you show gratitude, it is more than just being kind and pleasant...it is touching the heart of God. Saying thanks is a good word but showing gratitude is a great act. Do it while you can!

"We are bound to thank God always for you, brethren, as it is meet, because that your faith groweth exceedingly, and the charity of every one of you all toward each other aboundeth."
2 Thessalonians 1:3 (KJV)

EIGHTY-FIVE

Never settle for being a character in someone's story when you can write your own. Do not be distracted by temptations that cause you to settle for temporary pleasures and rob you of eternal blessings. Never go for less, just because you are too impatient to wait for the best. Do not settle for a life that is less than the one you are capable of living. When you accept the fact that your identity is found in Christ, you will never settle for less than the best. You are God's masterpiece, and you deserve the best!

"For we are His workmanship, created in Christ Jesus unto good works, which God hath before ordained that we should walk in them." Ephesians 2:10 (KJV)

EIGHTY-SIX

One of the most common and destructive habits that the enemy uses against us is the habit of worrying. There is a significant difference between worry and concern. A person who is worried sees a problem, and a concerned person solves the problem. Worry sends a message that we do not believe that God is big enough or able enough to take care of us. Worry is a weight that causes you to focus on problems instead of solutions. It robs today of the joy that is available and replaces it with sorrow. We should bring all our needs and concerns to God rather than worry about them. Worry is a purpose blocker.

"Casting all your care upon him; for He careth for you."
1 Peter 5:7 (KJV)

EIGHTY-SEVEN

Develop the discipline to wait on God. Too many times we suffer because we just could not wait for the manifestation of our prayers. Patience puts us in direct control of ourselves rather than getting hijacked by our emotions. Patience increases our threshold of tolerance so we can outlast the devil and prove ourselves faithful to God. Patience brings hope. When we are hopeful, we have a natural resilience and willingness to keep trying because we trust in God, and we are confident that God will keep his promises. Do not abort the victory. Wait upon God!

"But they that wait upon the LORD shall renew their strength; they shall mount up with wings as eagles; they shall run, and not be weary; and they shall walk, and not faint."
Isaiah 40:31 (KJV)

EIGHTY-EIGHT

Relationships suffer when there is no trust. When we trust someone, we have confidence in them and their honesty and integrity. We know that they will never take advantage of our vulnerability. Trust can be a fragile thing, but it is the foundation on which all relationships are built. Trust is earned when we see the character of God in a person—truthfulness, dependability, consistency, and reliability. When there is no trust, the foundation of the relationship is hypocrisy and abuse is inevitable. Be careful how we handle each other.

"Be kindly affectioned one to another with brotherly love; in honor preferring one another"
Romans 12:10 (KJV)

EIGHTY-NINE

It is better to remain silent and let people wonder if you are a fool than to talk and remove all doubt about it. Fine clothes and grand possessions may disguise ignorance, but silly words will always expose a fool. Only speak if it is going to improve the silence. Silence speaks volumes!

"Let your speech be always with grace, seasoned with salt, that ye may know how ye ought to answer every man." Colossians 4:6 (KJV)

NINETY

If your actions do not live up to your word, you have nothing to say. Do what is right not what is popular. When God gets the glory, truth is revealed. When self is glorified, truth is concealed.

"But be ye doers of the word, and not hearers only, deceiving your own selves." James 1:22 (KJV)

NINETY-ONE

Friends are those rare people who know when the thread gets broken how to tie a knot and get over the bump. Good friends are hard to find, difficult to leave, indelibly printed in your heart, and impossible to forget.

"A man that hath friends must shew himself friendly: and there is a friend that sticketh closer than a brother."
Proverbs 18:24 (KJV)

NINETY-TWO

Let your history with God guide you into your future with Him.

"Trust in the LORD with all thine heart; and lean not unto thine own understanding· In all thy ways acknowledge him, and he shall direct thy paths·" Proverbs 3:5-6 (KJV)

NINETY-THREE

The church is a hospital for those that are infected with the sin virus. The Blood of Jesus is the vaccine that washes and cleanses individuals and it guarantees healing and deliverance without side effects. The Blood that Jesus shed, way back on Calvary, will never lose its power and is effective with every variant of sin. It reaches the highest mountain and flows to the lowest valley. The Blood of Jesus is available to heal the sin-sick soul.

"How much more shall the blood of Christ, who through the eternal Spirit offered himself without spot to God, purge your conscience from dead works to serve the living God?" Hebrews 9:14 (KJV)

NINETY-FOUR

The best way to make a damaged machine work again is to break it down, work on the inner system, and fix the problem. Some bolts must be unscrewed to get to the broken places. There are times when we must unscrew the bolts of our lives, examine ourselves, and get rid of some things so that new things can be added. For progress to take place, the process of disassembly is sometimes necessary so we can reassemble our lives. Repackage your life and get going. Your season of brokenness will come to an end.

"But we all, with open face beholding as in a glass the glory of the Lord, are changed into the same image from glory to glory, even as by the Spirit of the Lord."
2 Corinthians 3:18 (KJV)

NINETY-FIVE

Do not ignore the little things in life. One day you may look back and realize they were the big things and they are all gone. Thankfulness turns what we have into enough, and more. Learn to appreciate and take note of the things you have. Gratefulness causes you to lose sight of the things that you lack. Be mindful of the people who make a difference in your life. Reflect upon your blessings and with a heart of gratitude say thanks to Almighty God!

"Rejoice evermore. Pray without ceasing. In everything give thanks: for this is the will of God in Christ Jesus concerning you."
1 Thessalonians 5:16-18 (KJV)

NINETY-SIX

If you have a 'WHY' to live for, God will show you 'HOW.' When your mind is arrested with the conviction to fulfill your purpose, your questions become your answers.

Why?

Why not?

Why not me?

Why not now?

"Let this mind be in you, which was also in Christ Jesus."
Philippians 2:5-6 (KJV)

NINETY-SEVEN

God has given you the power to re-establish your image, set new boundaries, refresh, start over with renewed values, and rebuild all that is broken in your life. Do not dwell on what went wrong. Instead, focus on what to do next. Overcome adversity by purposefully moving forward in faith. Recognize and accept when something has come to an end and be willing to start over. Walking away, shutting doors, finishing chapters, it does not matter what we call it; what matters is to leave the past behind. Your future is bright...go for it!

"Therefore if any man be in Christ, he is a new creature: old things are passed away; behold, all things are become new."
2 Corinthians 5:17 (KJV)

NINETY-EIGHT

A Destiny Helper is someone whom God has designated to assist you to fulfill your purpose in life. They do not necessarily wear special tags that identify them as destiny helpers, but you know them because they always push you in the right direction, push you to be your best, and add value to your life. They search for the right solutions and are always willing to help. They are ordinary men and women who wake up each morning and aim to make an impact in the lives of others. They are bathed in humility and never seek the spotlight. They walk with you and are never afraid to push you forward. May the divine help that is assigned to you locate you speedily.

"Behold, God is mine helper: the Lord is with them that uphold my soul." Psalm 54:4 (KJV)

NINETY-NINE

Your character is exposed not by where you sit on Sundays but by the actions you display all week. You do not have the right to hold somebody accountable for standards you refuse to apply yourself. If you wear a mask for too long, your face will eventually grow to fit it. Truth demands accountability, authenticity, and honesty!

"Thou hypocrite, first cast out the beam out of thine own eye; and then shalt thou see clearly to cast out the mote out of thy brother's eye." Matthew 7:5 (KJV)

ONE HUNDRED

Do not give up just because the situation is not ideal. There is no perfect situation. Even great relationships carry their own flaws. When you care enough, you will find a way to fix what is damaged or broken. The easy way out is to quit but do not take the easy way out. A relationship is like a house. When the roof leaks, you do not go and buy a new house ... you fix the roof.

"I returned, and saw under the sun, that the race is not to the swift, nor the battle to the strong, neither yet bread to the wise, nor yet riches to men of understanding, nor yet favor to men of skill; but time and chance happeneth to them all."
Ecclesiastes 9:11 (KJV)

ONE HUNDRED & ONE

Do not mistake respectability for holiness. There is a big difference. Respectability throws a blanket over sin and sweeps it under the rug where no one will see it -- out of sight out of mind. Holiness throws open the blinds and exposes our sin to us. It brings it into sight and convicts us to change.

"For God hath not called us unto uncleanness, but unto holiness."
1 Thessalonians 4:7 (KJV)

ONE HUNDRED & TWO

Stop crying over spilled milk. Do not focus on the problem. Focus on the solution. Learn from the mistake and change your mindset. You cannot solve your problems with the same thinking that created them.

"And be not conformed to this world: but be ye transformed by the renewing of your mind, that ye may prove what is that good, and acceptable, and perfect, will of God."
Romans 12:2 (KJV)

ONE HUNDRED & THREE

I am not just a survivor...I am more than a conqueror! Life is not simply to exist or to survive. It is to move ahead, ascend, overcome, endure, achieve, and conquer. It is being who God says I am.

"Nay, in all these things we are more than conquerors through him that loved us." Romans 8:37 (KJV)

ONE HUNDRED & FOUR

Recognize that time will never wait on you to get started. Time is a running factor; once it goes, it cannot be reclaimed. The clock ticks according to its own rhythm and its pre-determined purpose. Do not wait until everything is right. It will never be perfect. There will always be challenges, obstacles, and less-than-perfect conditions. So what? Get started now. Each step that you take will bring you closer to where you need to be. You will be wiser, better, stronger, and more equipped to succeed. Maximize your time!

"So teach us to number our days, that we may apply our hearts unto wisdom." Psalm 90:12 (KJV)

ONE HUNDRED & FIVE

Be careful who you allow to have access to you. Stay away from small-minded, jealous, insecure people who are always spewing venom and are always looking to you to validate them. Protect your space and your anointing.

"Be not deceived: evil communications corrupt good manners."
1 Corinthians 15:33 (KJV)

ONE HUNDRED & SIX

Your mind is fertile ground. It is the best piece of real estate you will ever own. Be careful to whom you lease it. Some tenants are just squatters who will destroy your property. Do not be afraid to give eviction notices. Exercise Mind Management!

"Finally, brethren, whatsoever things are true, whatsoever things are honest, whatsoever things are just, whatsoever things are pure, whatsoever things are lovely, whatsoever things are of good report; if there be any virtue, and if there be any praise, think on these things." Philippians 4:8 (KJV)

ONE HUNDRED & SEVEN

Life presents us a smorgasbord of trials and uncertainties. God allows us to go through some rough places, hills, and valleys. Daily we must dig deep within ourselves to find the strength to cope. Amazingly with each trial we get stronger and better. Through it all, God holds us and steers us to a higher ground. He never leaves us nor forsakes us. He carries us when we can no longer carry ourselves. He is our great deliverer!

"But the God of all grace, who hath called us unto his eternal glory by Christ Jesus, after that ye have suffered a while, make you perfect, stablish, strengthen, settle you."
1 Peter 5:10 (KJV)

ONE HUNDRED & EIGHT

You are responsible for the circle you create. Be around people who make you want to be a better person. Do not hang out with naysayers and those who can only see the glass as half empty. Be steadfast on your journey to greatness and be not distracted by foolishness. Focus on your mission, be resolute in your pursuit of excellence, and always do the right thing.

"He that walketh with wise men shall be wise: but a companion of fools shall be destroyed."
Proverbs 13:20 (KJV)

ONE HUNDRED & NINE

Let your life inspire others to dream more and to be better than they are. Do not follow the path that has already been charted. Be the one to blaze the path and leave the trail for others to follow. Dare to be different so you can make a difference!

"Let your light so shine before men, that they may see your good works, and glorify your Father which is in heaven." Matthew 5:16 (KJV)

ONE HUNDRED & TEN

It is only after you have stepped outside your comfort zone that you begin to change, grow, and transform. Life is a series of natural and spontaneous changes, but the greatest change is when your mind is changed. It is a process that allows you to improve and evolve. Those who cannot change their minds cannot change anything. If you remain a caterpillar, you will always crawl. If you become a butterfly, you will fly and never crawl again.

"And be not conformed to this world: but be ye transformed by the renewing of your mind, that ye may prove what is that good, and acceptable, and perfect, will of God."
Romans 12:2 (KJV)

ONE HUNDRED & ELEVEN

Stop comparing yourself with others. Celebrate your uniqueness. You have your distinct assignment from God. The sun and the moon give light but there is no comparison between them. They shine when it is their time according to their purpose.

"For we dare not make ourselves of the number or compare ourselves with some that commend themselves: but they measuring themselves by themselves, and comparing themselves among themselves, are not wise."
2 Corinthians 10:12 (KJV)

ONE HUNDRED & TWELVE

Foolishness keeps you stuck in your past. Wisdom opens the door to your future. Whatever choices you make today will build or destroy your tomorrow.
Choose wisely!

"The way of a fool is right in his own eyes: but he that hearkened unto counsel is wise."
Proverbs 12:15 (KJV)

ONE HUNDRED & THIRTEEN

Being rich is not defined by what you get but it is by what you give. When you give more to others than they give to you, what you have given will find its way back to you. By helping others to get what they want, you make a great investment in yourself. Help someone today!

"But this I say, He which soweth sparingly shall reap also sparingly; and he which soweth bountifully shall reap also bountifully. Every man according as he purposeth in his heart, so let him give; not grudgingly, or of necessity: for God loveth a cheerful giver. And God is able to make all grace abound toward you..." 2 Corinthians 9:6-8 (KJV)

113

ONE HUNDRED & FOURTEEN

Get started! Do not wait until everything is perfect. If you wait for all the lights to turn green, you will never get to your destination. You have everything you need to make an impact in the world if you can get past your excuses. Stop questioning yourself. Stop listening to everyone else. God is waiting for you to start what He has already finished.

"Being confident of this very thing, that he which hath begun a good work in you will perform it until the day of Jesus Christ."
Philippians 1:6 (KJV)

ONE HUNDRED & FIFTEEN

To be the best you, you must always excuse yourself from the presence of shallow-minded people. Mediocrity knows nothing higher than itself. Do what the majority of people do, and you will end up being a slave to mediocrity. Take the road less traveled and shoot for excellence. Eagles are distinctive in their realm of operation. An eagle's flight path is never low, and it never flies with pigeons. Take the high road!

"Enter ye in at the strait gate: for wide is the gate, and broad is the way, that leadeth to destruction, and many there be which go in thereat." Matthew 7:13 (KJV)

ONE HUNDRED & SIXTEEN

Learn to dismiss those things that are not relevant and not adding value to your life. Love reveals itself by the actions of those who profess to be carriers. You never have to speculate if someone loves you. Love is evident in its presentation. Do not waste moments waiting and wondering. Do not throw away your time dreaming of someone that does not want you. No one is that amazing, certainly not the one who would pass you up.
Move on!

"My little children, let us not love in word, neither in tongue; but in deed and in truth."
1 John 3:18 (KJV)

ONE HUNDRED & SEVENTEEN

Stop allowing negative people to dilute or poison your day with their words or opinions. Do not allow negative people to speak over your life. When they tell you that roses have thorns; tell them you are grateful that thorns have roses. The thorns teach you how to navigate your way through the ups and downs of life. With each prick, you see the BLOOD!

"Be not deceived: evil communications corrupt good manners." 1 Corinthians 15:33

ONE HUNDRED & EIGHTEEN

Do not waste time living someone else's life. Do not let the noise of other people's opinions drown out your own inner voice. Release yourself from being governed by the mindset of others.

"The fear of man bringeth a snare: but whoso putteth his trust in the LORD shall be safe."
Proverbs 29:25 (KJV)

ONE HUNDRED & NINETEEN

Bitterness is a heavy weight that ushers in inertia and leaves you stuck in the misery of yesterday. Do not give bitterness an occupancy lease in your heart. Serve it an eviction notice and replace it with forgiveness. Bitterness is an anchor that ties you to failure. It is a venom that consumes its host and shrinks the capacity to evolve into a better version of self. When you harbor grudges and suppress anger, you leave the door open for bitterness to enter in your life. Bitterness puts you in a self-imposed prison where you are sentenced to relive the hurt and pain of your past over and over. It is a weight so heavy that obliterates joy and shackles you to a life of misery and defeat.

"Looking diligently lest any man fail of the grace of God; lest any root of bitterness springing up trouble you, and thereby many be defiled."
Hebrews 12:15 (KJV)

ONE HUNDRED & TWENTY

Your now is preparing you for your next. Be ready for the new chapter of your life to begin. God has a great future destined for you. A shift is coming!

"For I know the thoughts that I think toward you, saith the LORD, thoughts of peace, and not of evil, to give you an expected end."
Jeremiah 29:11 (KJV)

EPILOGUE

Do not just exist.
Live
Get out
Explore
Laugh
Evolve
Learn
Serve
Love
Let God be pleased with you.
Be all that you can be.
Live life to the fullest.
Enjoy life there is plenty of time to be dead!

"Thou wilt shew me the path of life: in thy presence is fulness of joy; at thy right hand there are pleasures for evermore."
Psalm 16:11 (KJV)

About The Author

ANGELA MARIE RUCKER, Th.D., D.D.

Dr. Angela Rucker is an international minister and lecturer.

Travelling extensively throughout the world, Dr. Rucker ministers restoration to people who are broken and void of purpose.   Dr. Rucker deals with the real issues of life and presents an alternative to all of life struggles. The focus of her ministry is to empower people to walk in Dominion and maximize God's purpose for their lives.

Dr. Rucker serves as the Assistant Pastor of Bride of Christ Church Ministries International located in Mitchellville, MD. USA. She is the President and Chief executive Officer of Cradle of H.O.P.E. Foundation which is a humanitarian organization that serves underprivileged children all over the world.

Dr. Rucker earned a Doctorate in Theology from Andersonville Theological Seminary. She was awarded an Honorary Doctorate in Divinity from Eastern North Carolina Theological Institute. Being the consummate scholar, she earned a Ph.D. in Pastoral Counseling from Empowerment Theological Institute and Bible Seminary.

Dr. Rucker and her husband, Dr. Benjamin, serve together as a team. They are called to go beyond geographical boundaries to teach and preach the uncompromising word of God. They travel together and plant many churches on different continents.

Made in the USA
Middletown, DE
18 February 2023

25054772R00073